Scholastic Phonics

How Jigsaws Are Made

Published in the UK by Scholastic Education, 2023
Scholastic Distribution Centre, Bosworth Avenue, Tournament Fields, Warwick, CV34 6UQ
Scholastic Ireland, 89E Lagan Road, Dublin Industrial Estate, Glasnevin, Dublin, D11 HP5F

SCHOLASTIC and associated logos are trademarks and/or registered trademarks of Scholastic Inc.
www.scholastic.co.uk
© 2023 Scholastic
1 2 3 4 5 6 7 8 9   3 4 5 6 7 8 9 0 1 2

Printed by Ashford Colour Press
The book is made of materials from well-managed, FSC®-certified forests and other controlled sources.

A CIP catalogue record for this book is available from the British Library.
ISBN 978-0702-32108-5

All rights reserved. This book is sold subject to the condition that it shall not, by way of trade or otherwise, be lent, hired out or otherwise circulated in any form of binding or cover other than that in which it is published. No part of this publication may be reproduced, stored in a retrieval system, or transmitted in any form or by any other means (electronic, mechanical, photocopying, recording or otherwise) without prior written permission of Scholastic.

Every effort has been made to trace copyright holders for the works reproduced in this publication, and the publishers apologise for any inadvertent omissions.

Author
Suzy Ditchburn
Editorial team
Rachel Morgan, Vicki Yates, Caroline Hale, Jennie Clifford
Design team
Dipa Mistry, Andrea Lewis, We Are Grace
Illustrations
Alex Oxton/Advocate Art
Photographs
p1, 4 Gorlov/iStock
p5 Public Domain, from the British Library's collections, 2013 made available under the Creative Commons CC0 1.0 Universal Public Domain Dedication/WikimediaCommons
p6–7, 22–23 Monkey Business Images/Shutterstock
p3, 8–9 MNStudio/Shutterstock

Help your child to read!

This book practises these letters and letter sounds.
Point and say the sounds with your child:

- o (as in 'go')
- i (as in 'find')
- a–e (as in 'made')
- i–e (as in 'size')
- aw (as in 'jigsaw')

Your child may need help to read these common tricky words:

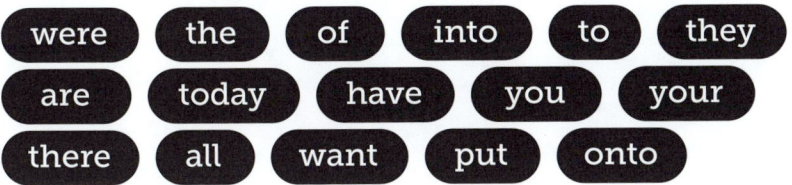

- were
- the
- of
- into
- to
- they
- are
- today
- have
- you
- your
- there
- all
- want
- put
- onto

Before reading
- Look at the cover picture and read the title together. Read the back cover blurb to your child.
- Ask your child: *Do you like puzzles? Have you ever done a jigsaw?*
- Talk about the image in the magnifying glass.

During reading
- If your child gets stuck on a word, remind them to sound it out and then blend the sounds to read the word: j-i-g-s-aw, jigsaw.
- If they are still stuck, show them how to read the word.
- Enjoy looking at the pictures together. Pause to talk about the information.

After reading
- Talk about the images on page 24. What can your child tell you about them?
- Ask your child: *Do they laminate the jigsaw before or after they put the picture on thick card?*
- Discuss with your child their favourite part of the book. Ask them to explain why they liked it.

Jigsaws were invented over 250 years ago in the United Kingdom.

A mapmaker pasted a map on a flat bit of wood and then cut it into segments with a thin saw.

Jigsaws were used to educate children, and they still are today.

They became popular with children and adults.

Have you ever completed a jigsaw? They are good for your mind and can help you unwind.

There are lots of jigsaw sizes. The biggest jigsaws have thousands of segments!

Let's find out how jigsaws are made.

1. First of all you need a drawing.

2. Then this is made into a computer drawing.

3. The chosen drawing is then printed on paper.

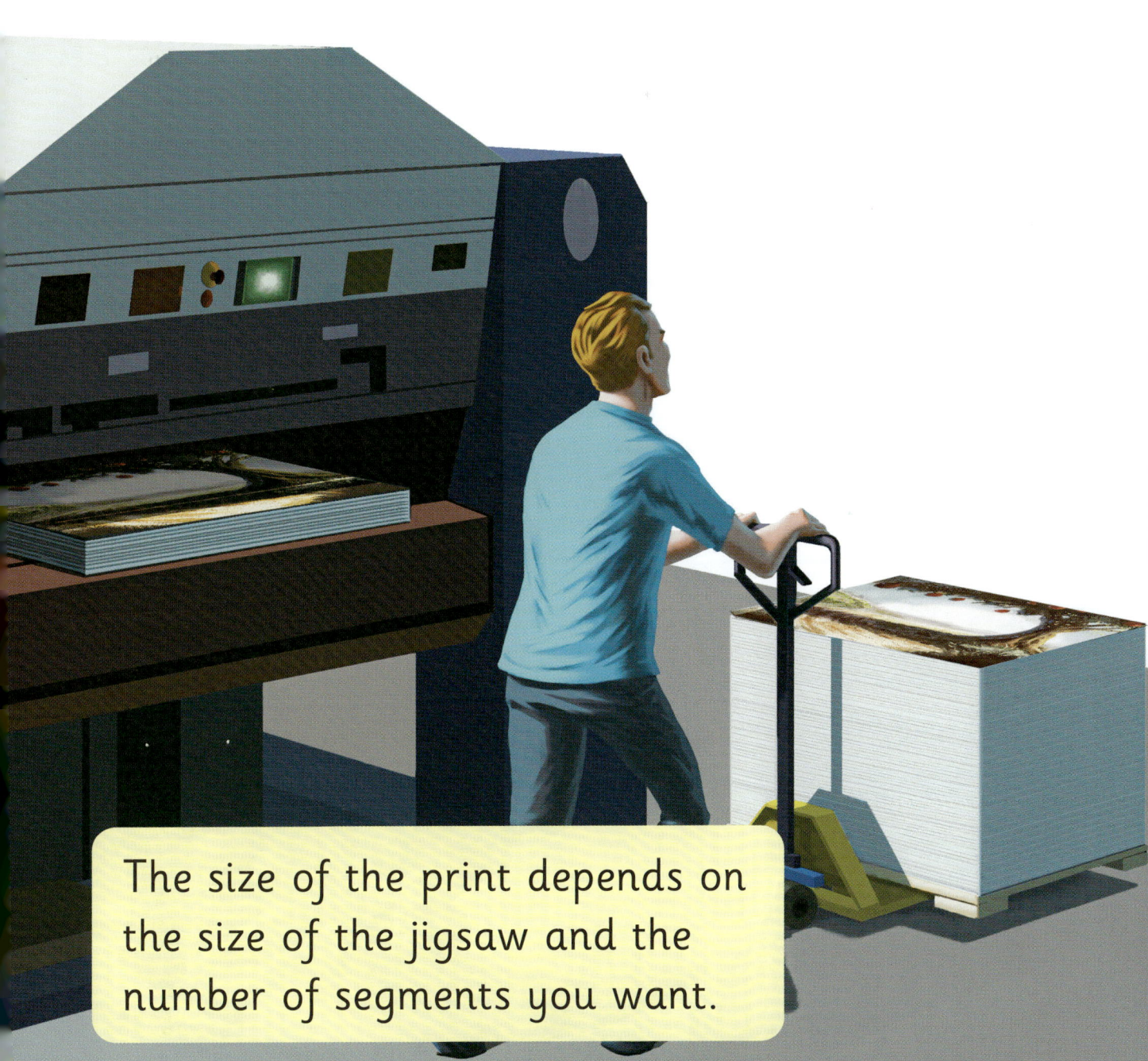

The size of the print depends on the size of the jigsaw and the number of segments you want.

4. The print is then put on thick card or a kind of wood made from sawdust and woodchips.

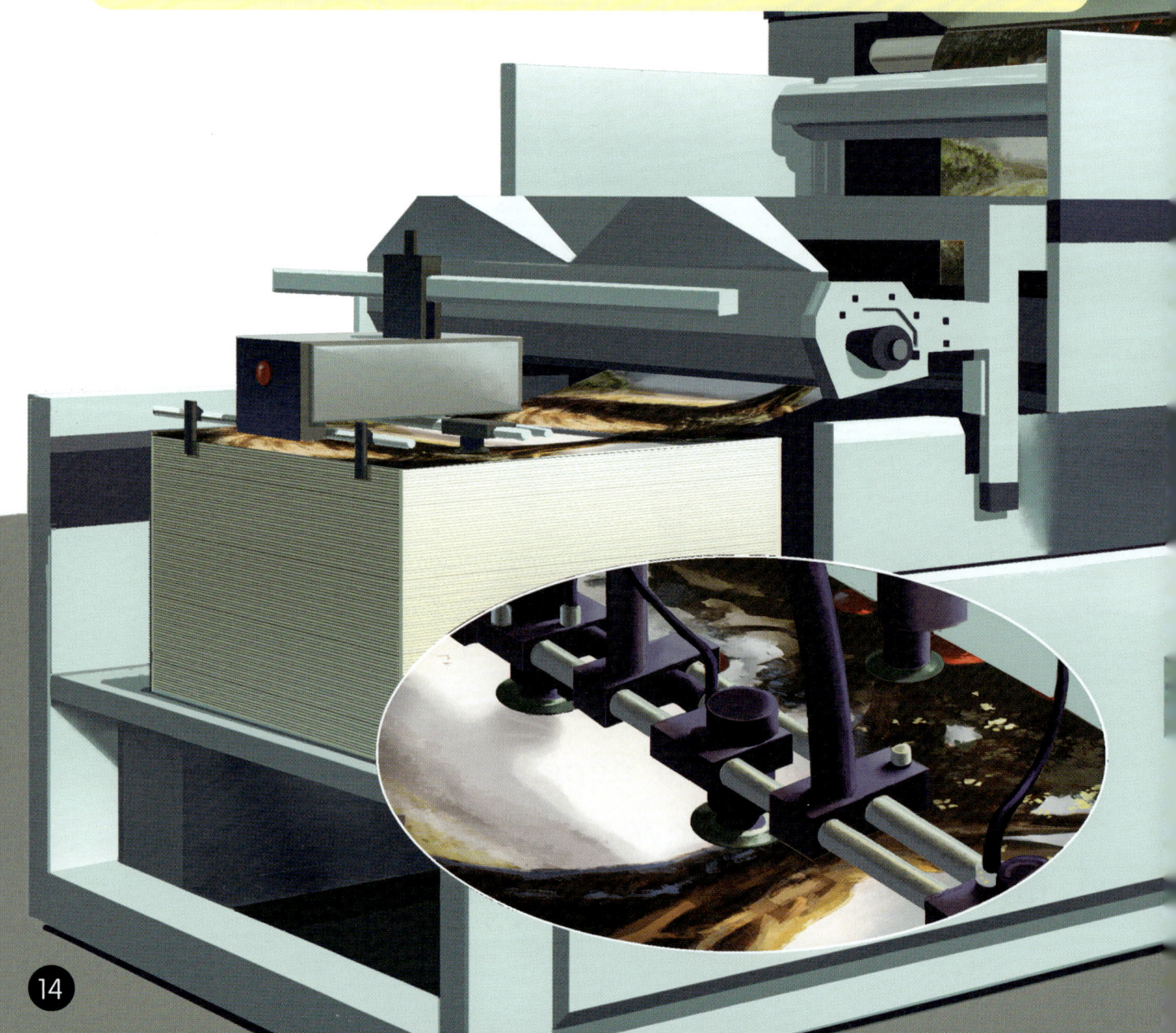

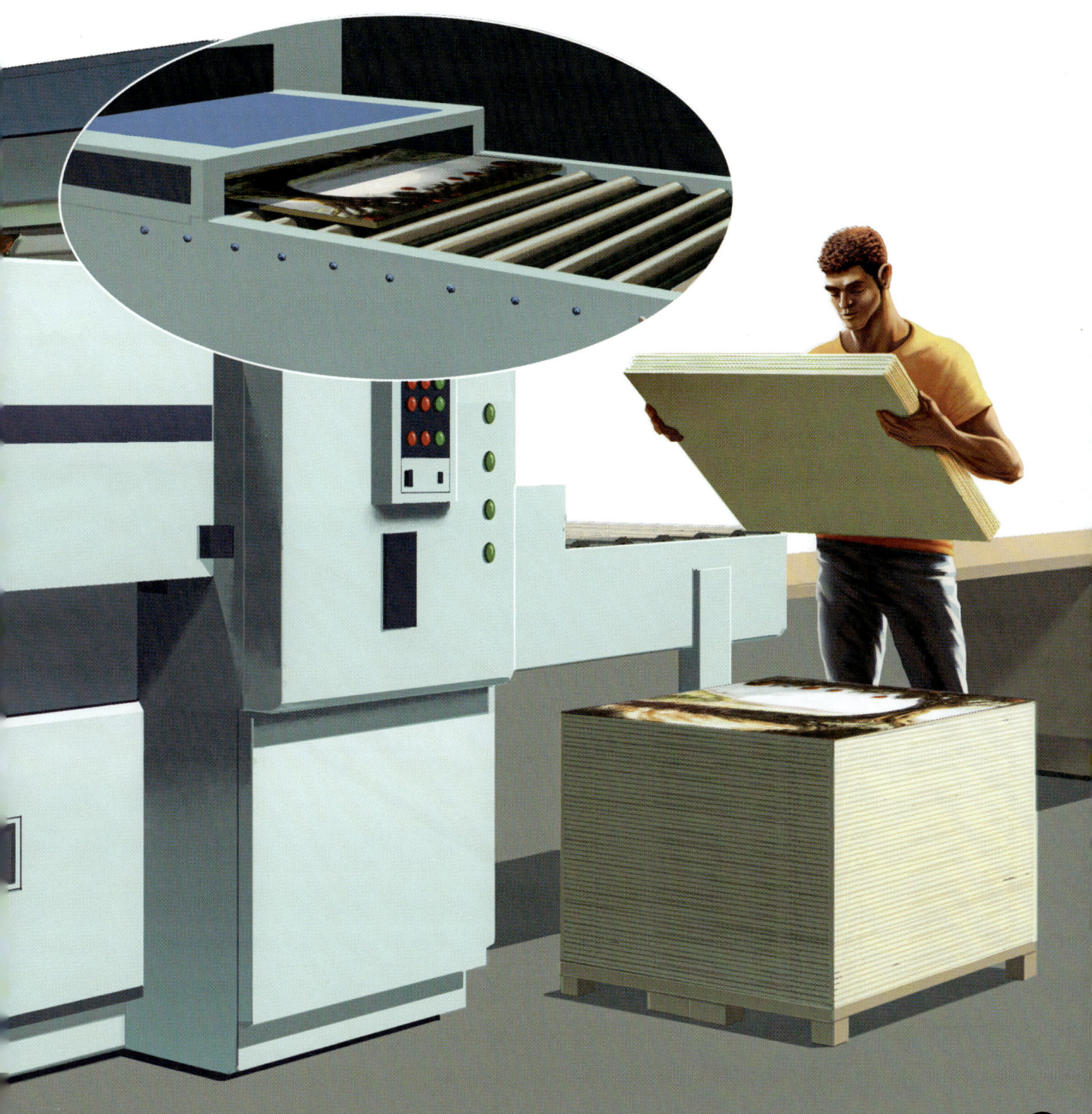

5. Next the jigsaw needs to be laminated with a clear film coating to protect it.

It is set aside until it dries.

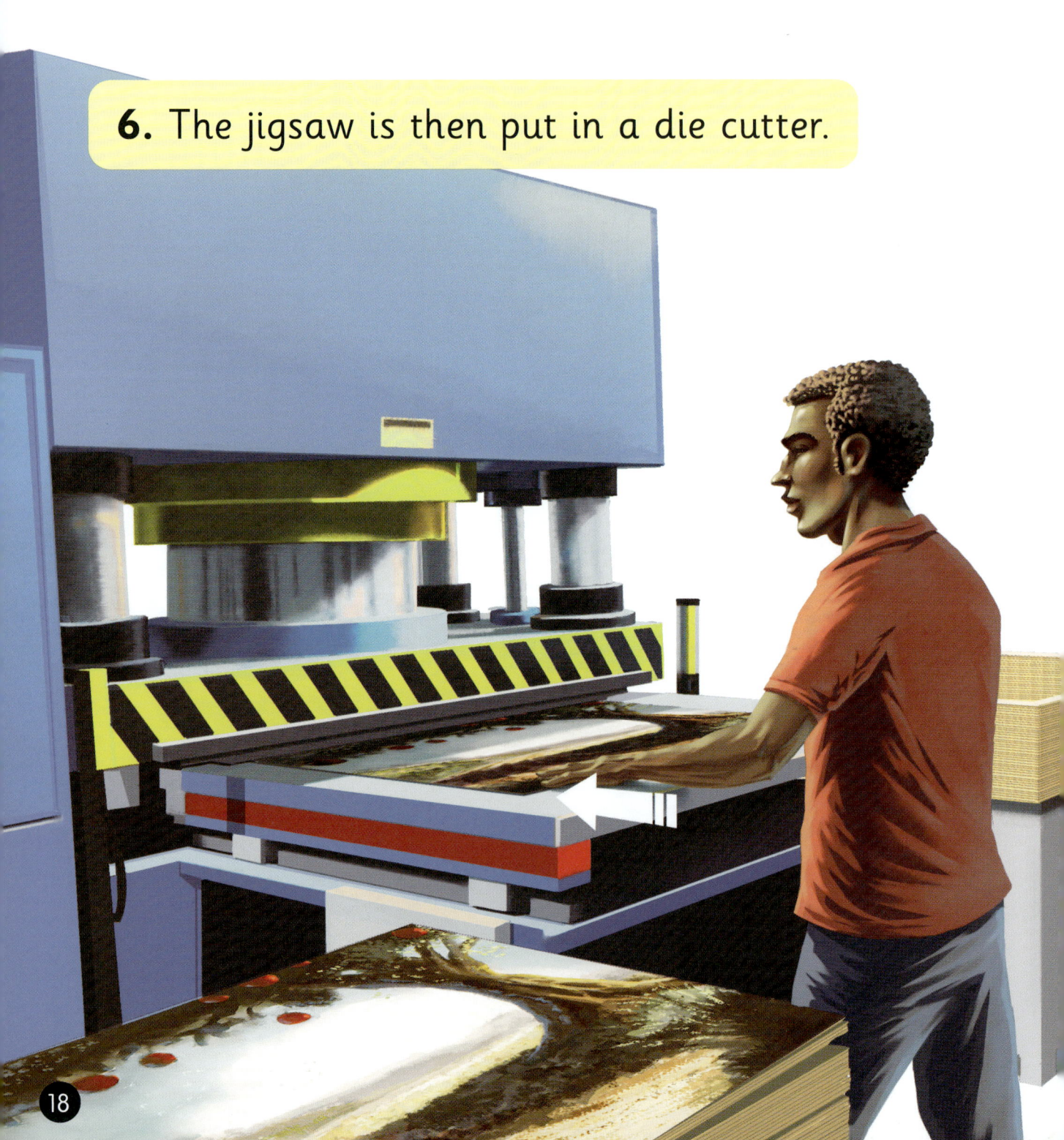
6. The jigsaw is then put in a die cutter.

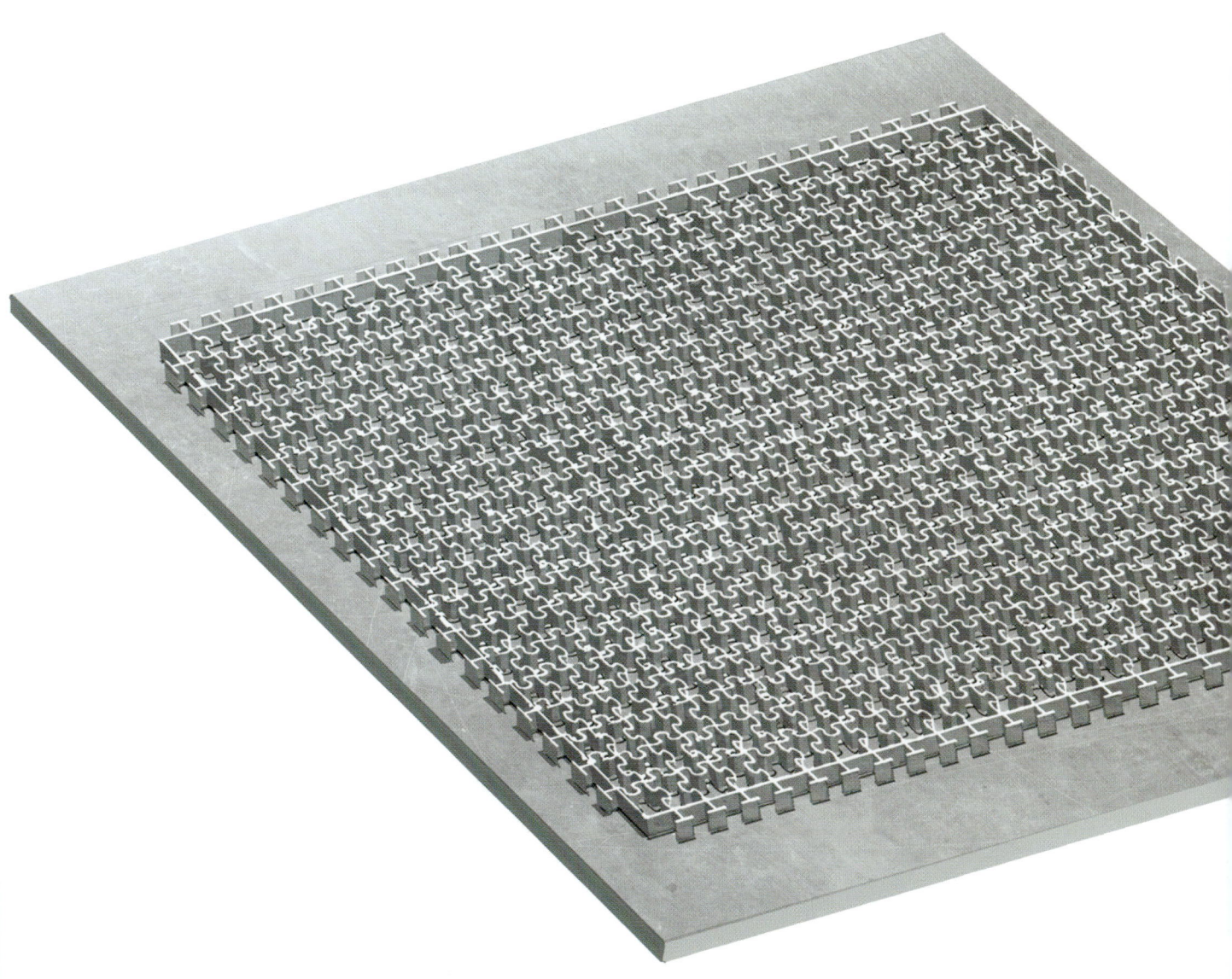

It is like a cookie cutter that cuts the drawing into segments.

7. The jigsaw is put in a box and sent to a customer or shop.

The box lid has the same drawing as the jigsaw, to help you complete it.

Now it's time to have a go at completing the jigsaw. Pick a segment and find the shape it fits onto. Keep going and soon you will have finished it!

Talk about it!